# Traditional Hymn Favorites

## 10 SACRED PIANO SOLOS

### Arranged by Carolyn C. Setliff

ISBN 978-1-5400-9761-3

WILLIS MUSIC

EXCLUSIVELY DISTRIBUTED BY

HAL•LEONARD®

Visit Hal Leonard Online at
**www.halleonard.com**

Contact us:
**Hal Leonard**
7777 West Bluemound Road
Milwaukee, WI 53213
Email: info@halleonard.com

In Europe, contact:
**Hal Leonard Europe Limited**
42 Wigmore Street
Marylebone, London, W1U 2RN
Email: info@halleonardeurope.com

In Australia, contact:
**Hal Leonard Australia Pty. Ltd.**
4 Lentara Court
Cheltenham, Victoria, 3192 Australia
Email: info@halleonard.com.au

# All Creatures of Our God and King

Traditional German
*Arr. Carolyn C. Setliff*

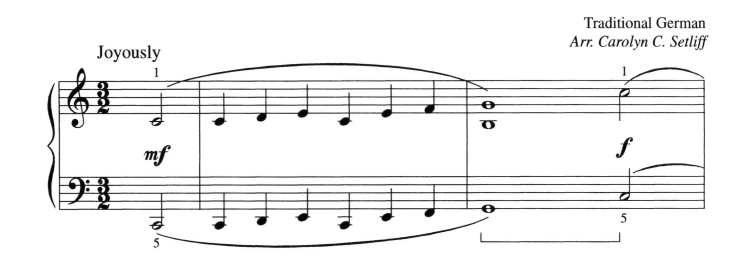

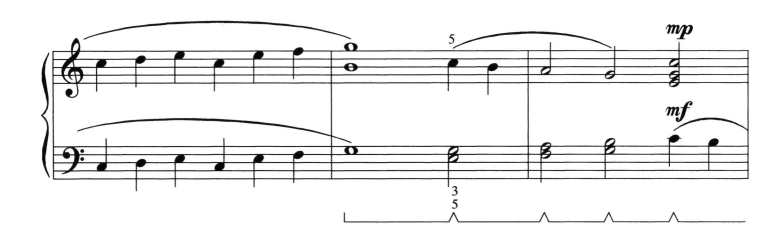

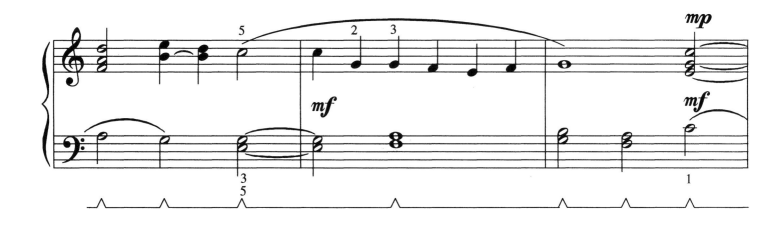

# Dona Nobis Pacem

Traditional Latin
*Arr. Carolyn C. Setliff*

# Joyful, Joyful, We Adore Thee

Ludwig van Beethoven
*Arr. Carolyn C. Setliff*

# Tallis Canon

Thomas Tallis
*Arr. Carolyn C. Setliff*

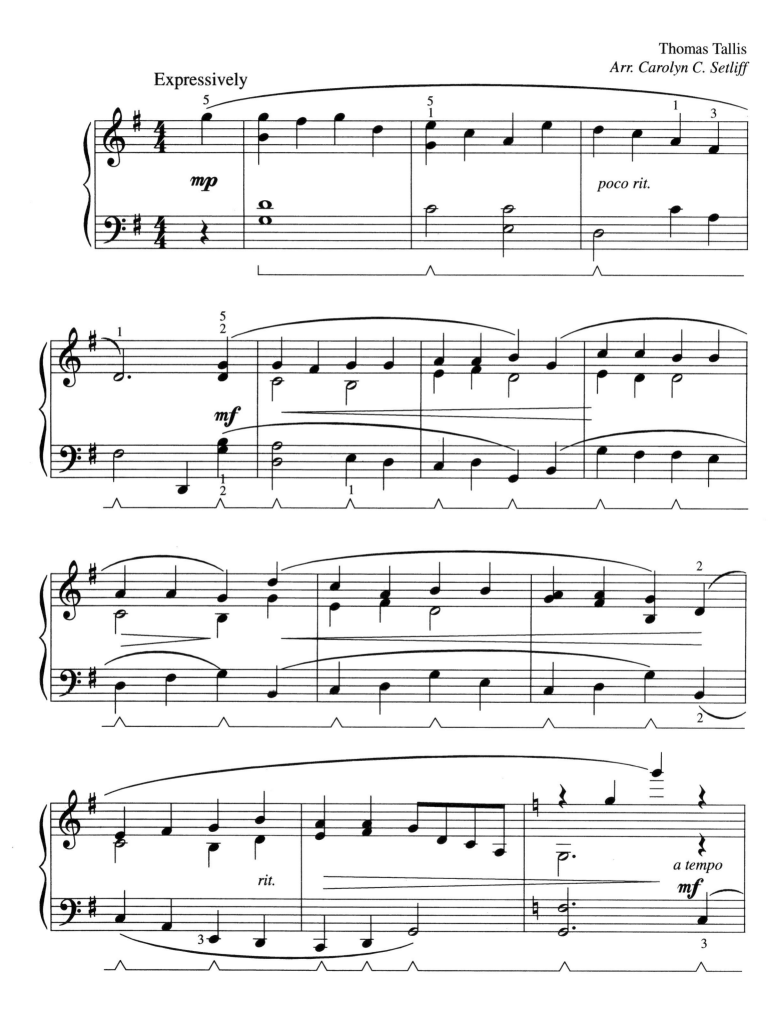

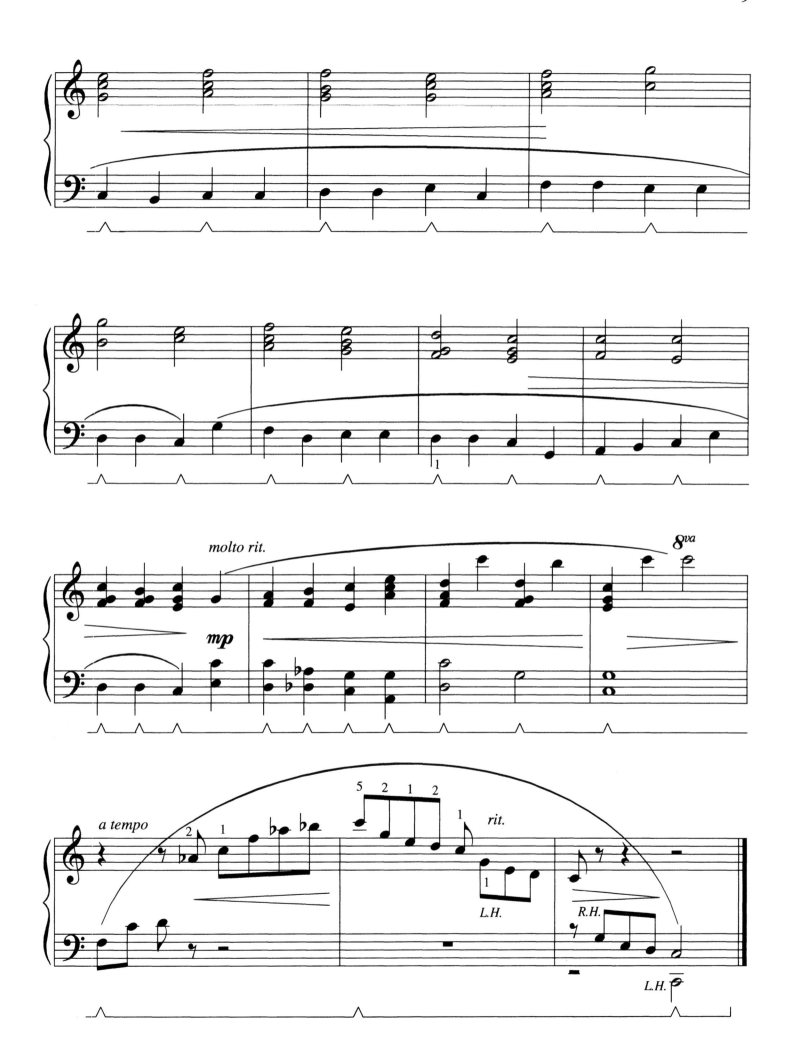

# I Sing the Mighty Power of God

Traditional English Melody
*Arr. Carolyn C. Setliff*

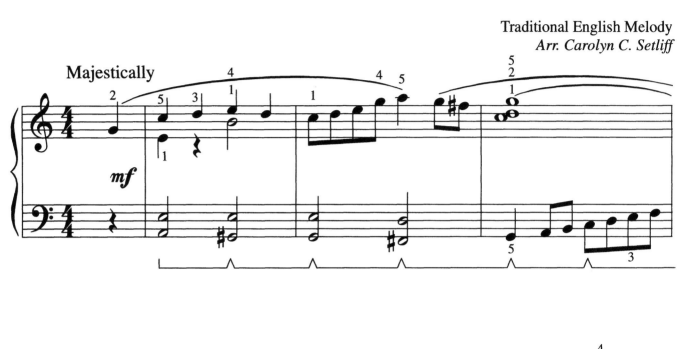

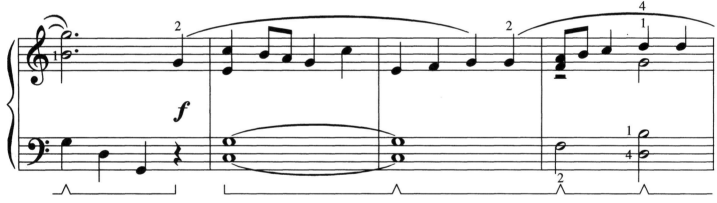

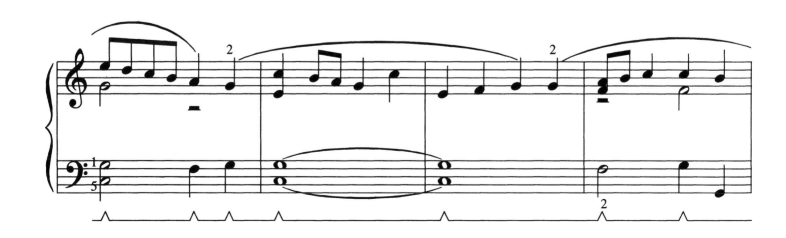

# Onward Christian Soldiers

Arthur S. Sullivan
*Arr. Carolyn C. Setliff*

# All Things Bright and Beautiful

17th Century English
*Arr. Carolyn C. Setliff*

# Come, Thou Fount of Every Blessing

John Wyeth
*Arr. Carolyn C. Setliff*

# Come, Christians, Join to Sing

Traditional Melody
*Arr. Carolyn C. Setliff*

Joyously

# This Little Light of Mine

American Spiritual
*Arr. Carolyn C. Setliff*

*no pedal*